CW01622087

Here Comes Cocoa

Written by Deborah Jane

Illustrated by Mischa Pearson

Copyright © 2023 by Deborah Jane Cooper

All rights reserved.

No portion of this book may be reproduced in any form without written permission from the publisher or author, except as permitted by U.S. copyright law.

Dedication

For my darling husband and children – your love fills every page and memory of this book. For Emily, whose light and spirit will forever be a reminder of the fun and warmth she brought into our lives. Not forgetting Cocoa, our faithful companion, whose presence remains an irreplaceable part of our family's story. Forever loved and forever cherished.

About the Author

Writing a children's book has been a long-standing dream of mine since my children were young. Reading books like Famous Five and The Magic Faraway Tree to them inspired me to write about the adventures my family had with our beloved puppy Cocoa. The amount of joy a single puppy can bring is surprising. The incredible adventures we had and the trouble she got into were beyond anything I could have imagined. As humans and dogs developed friendships, an abundance of real-life stories surfaced, bringing both moments of joy and of sadness.

The following story is grounded in real-life events, with every chapter recounting an actual adventure. It has been a joy to write this book, giving you a glimpse into our family and, above all, Cocoa. I hope you enjoy reading it as much as I enjoyed writing it. I am thankful in abundance to Mishca Pearson, the incredible illustrator – without who my dream would not have become reality. You've captured our family perfectly.

Deborah Jane

For Molly

I hope you enjoy cheeky Cocoa's antics.

With love

Deborah Jane B

Contents

Chapter One

Back to School

The onset of a new day at Meaburn Hill Farm was marked by the arrival of beautiful sunshine. The apple trees in the orchard swayed as a gentle breeze blew, dropping some apples and bringing joy to the hungry crows observing. With the days growing shorter, the family cherished the remaining weeks of daylight. Before the children returned from school, Vicky hung up the laundry in the garden and took out a fresh loaf from the oven. It had been two weeks since the summer holidays had finished. Coming back from a tiring day, Sam and Sarah would be delighted to find fresh bread and delicious cheese waiting for them at home. Fresh air smells wafted through the house thanks to the open top half of the creaky sky blue stable door.

"Not too many more lovely sunny days like this, I don't expect," Vicky said to herself. She loved this last hour of peace, before the family all started bustling through the door, wanting this and that, throwing their school bags and jumpers in a heap on the cloakroom floor for all to fall over. It must be said that Albert wasn't any better than the children, often forgetting to remove his boots and leaving muddy footprints in the kitchen after working on the farm all day. Vicky's rolling eyes always vanished when the children hugged her and excitedly chatted about their day, and a tender kiss on her head from Albert. After a quick cup of tea, he would be back out in the fields until suppertime. There was still so much to do before the winter.

It was an exceptionally exciting day today. Today was the day the children would finally get to see the puppies of Jess, the golden labrador up the lane, for the very first time. Laura Carr, Jess' human, was a fantastic friend of Vicky's. She didn't have any children of her own, so adored Sam and Sarah going to visit.

The conversation during breakfast that morning was filled with amusement.

"You're only going to *visit* the puppies." Albert declared, as he ate the final slice of jammy toast. "Do not be coming home with any ideas!"

"Of course, Dad!" they all replied, including Vicky, with a giggle and a smile at her husband. With a disapproving expression, Albert returned to the farm, muttering under his breath about dogs being meant for outdoor work.

Just as the bread was taken from the oven, the clock chimed through the house as it struck three. Vicky had a ten-minute heads-up to get ready for her two energetic children rushing in. They had both grown so much over the summer. Now nine, Sam was becoming taller and more like his dad, showing a keen interest in the farm and its workings. Sarah, who recently celebrated her seventh birthday, was a lively girl who loved to help Mummy in the kitchen. Her favourite thing to do was run her finger around the bowl of an uncooked cake mix and lick every last drop off her little fingers. Vicky hoped and prayed they would never change.

Both children enjoyed their piano lessons, but getting them to practice during the week was always a challenge. However, once the music filled the air, the whole house would come alive. With a tablecloth floating behind her, Sarah danced and imagined herself as a princess getting married, while Sam played the black and white keys – Sam sometimes having to pretend to be the fortunate prince, which was starting to become embarrassing for the nine-year-old. What if the boys at school found out? Little did he know that they all had dreamy little sisters too.

"Mum, I'm famished!" Vicky's thoughts were interrupted as Sam dashed through the back door, sliding his new satchel across the cloak room floor, gathering a few pairs of shoes on its way before coming to a stop with a thud at the sideboard.

"Where's your sister?" Vicky asked, taking a deep breath and trying to ignore the scratches developing on his new bag.

"Oh, she's floating up the lane, slowly, dreaming of being a mermaid or something. Here she is now."

Sarah made a dramatic entrance into the kitchen, flapping her arms like fins as she swam through the door. She then sat down on the stool next to the freshly baked loaf, keeping her pink glittery rucksack on her back. The rucksack had been a birthday present from her "bestest best friend" Emily.

"Mmmm, Mummy, that smells de-wish-us," she exclaimed, sucking in the doughy aroma.

"It's delicious," sighed her big brother. "The word is delicious."

"That's what I said!" she replied with her hands on her hips, "De-wi-shus!"

Sam grunted and walked over to the bread, reaching to tear a piece off.

"Er, not so fast Mister!" shouted Vicky, "Both go and wash your hands and I will slice you some bread. There may be some apples from the garden to go with the cheese, if you're lucky." The children ran out of the kitchen, still disputing the word 'delicious' and whether or not mermaids were real. Both children were fortunate to have their own separate rooms. Some of their friends had to share with their siblings. Sam's room was decorated with space rocket wallpaper and superhero posters, with Spiderman as his favourite. To sum it up, the room was impressively clean for a boy on the verge of entering high school. In the corner, an old PlayStation collected dust, reserved for weekends when his friend Ben came over to play. However, Sarah was the complete opposite of tidy. Teddies, clothes, and glittery, feathery bits and bobs from the craft box hid the beautiful autumn-coloured wooden floor. The chosen yellow wallpaper was decorated with posters of dogs and Hello Kitty, according to her preference. Resting on the dressing table was a frame that had a picture of her school friends, Emily and Anna, playfully sticking their tongues out.

After a couple of minutes, both kids came running back to the kitchen and were handed plates of yummy snacks. Sam took a sneaky peek at Sarah's plate to check she hadn't got more cheese than him. Cheese being Sam's absolute favourite thing to eat.

"I'm so excited to be going to see the new puppies, Mummy," said Sarah with a grin from ear to ear. "Do you think we will be able to hold them and cuddle them?"

"I am sure we can darling, but remember what Daddy said: we are just looking!" Vicky knew how much Sarah loved puppies. Emily, her best friend, had three dogs. Sarah just loved to lie on the floor when she went for a play date, while they all walked and drooled all over her.

"You are one crazy dog lover, Sarah," Emily would say. "If you keep letting the dogs lick you like that, you'll start barking soon."

Sam sighed and shook his head as Sarah loudly chomped on the apple and cheese sandwich she had made. In his mind, he considered the strange combination. As he stretched on the stool and tried to tune out the loud noise from her eating, he stated firmly, "Mum, I don't want to cuddle the puppies. I will just stroke them now that I am so much older than Sarah."

"That's OK Sam," grinned his mum, knowing full well her little 'big' boy still snuggled up to his toy tiger in bed each night.

Just as the discussion was taking place, in strolled Albert, kicking off his muddy boots, looking forward to his cup of tea and some sticky strawberry jam and bread. He planted a kiss on his wife's head, her unruly blonde curls forming a mound, before taking a seat in his beloved chair next to the cosy oven.

"We are soooo excited, Daddy!" cried Sarah. "We are going to see the new golden puppies at Mrs Carr's cottage."

"Oh yes, so you are," replied an anxious Albert. "Remember, you are just looking."

"I've got this, Dad," Sam chimed in, hoping to show his father his newfound sense of responsibility and adulthood.

"Eat up your snacks and then go and get changed out of your school uniforms while I finish prepping tea. Then we'll head over to Laura's to see the pups." Both children shovelled the remaining bits of bread into their hungry mouths and then ran from the kitchen, up the wooden staircase, to follow their mum's instructions.

As Vicky prepared the potatoes and other vegetables, she thought of her family who'd been chatting and eating. Could there be time to make an apple pie, maybe? Apple pie was Albert's favourite pudding, especially with lashings of piping hot custard. Her love for these individuals, she was proud to call her family, was immense. Her life and home were complete .... or so she thought.

Chapter Two

An Exciting Visit

"Is it okay if we bring some sweets for the puppies? Sarah hurriedly sat on the floor and quickly put on her trainers, extending her feet for assistance in tying her shoelaces. He was incredibly skilled at tying laces, her brother. She looked up at him, beaming at how clever he was as he looped and pulled her pink glittery laces.

"Puppies don't eat sweets," sighed Sam. His little sister had a lot to learn.

"That's correct, they have no taste for sweets, but they might find comfort in a new blanket or teddy bear to cuddle. How about choosing one of your teddies to give as a gift to them?" said Vicky, as she hunted under the messy pile of damp tea towels for her car keys.

Sarah hurriedly climbed back up the stairs, or wooden hills as her dad would call them, her purple-soled and pink-laced shoes loudly stomping. Minutes later, she returned with a white, cuddly rabbit she had owned since she was a baby.

"I think the puppies would like to cuddle up to my bunny, Snowdrop," she announced. "Snowdrop is very good at giving cuddles."

"Found the keys, Mum," yelled Sam from the pantry. "They were under the butter-dish lid."

"Oh, how did they get there?" Vicky looked confused. "Never mind, let's go."

Smiling to herself and appearing slightly flushed, Sarah continued on without confessing to hiding the keys in the pantry. The keys to the Princess' tower couldn't be left in the kitchen for the wicked witch to discover, right?

Sam imagined the day he could drive himself while sitting in the front of his mum's bottle green Land Rover. He loved cars.

"When I'm old enough, I'm going to buy my own car," he announced proudly. "Then I'll be able to drive us to exciting places." He held out his hands and pretended to turn the imaginary steering wheel, pursing his lips and making a "brumming" noise as they continued down the lane. Dad allowed him to shift gears and even let him drive down the farm track before reaching the main road, when Mum and Sarah were not in the car, avoiding Eric Manwaring's gaze.

Eric Manwaring was the village on-foot police officer - the only one left for several miles. He was firm, but fair and kind. Everybody loved him. His wife, Susan, owned the sweet shop on the corner and would stand outside, letting children try new sweet samples as they passed on their way home from school. She was also the local Sunday School teacher. She had a beautiful singing voice and would enjoy singing and teaching the songs in church each Sunday, while Eric would hand out and collect in the hymn books at the doors.

"Here we are," announced Vicky. "Now, when I say it's time to leave, we have to leave. Right, Sarah?"

“Yes, Mummy. I promise,” Sarah jumped down out of the back seat, straight into a thick, black muddy puddle. The purple pumps with pink laces were no longer purple and pink.

“Oops!" Sarah glanced up at her mother with her eyes wide and biting her bottom lip. “Sorrrr-rryyyy!” she drawled.

Sighing, Vicky grabbed her daughter’s hand and led her to Laura Carr’s back door. “Not to worry, just kick off your shoes as you go inside.”

As Mum had given him the task of locking the car, Sam trailed behind. He clicked the lock and popped the keys into his pocket, swaggering toward the house and pretending to be a proper driver.

Opening the back door of her charming cottage, Laura began to clap her hands in excitement and exclaimed with enthusiasm.

"Come on inside everyone!"

Laura, as well as her love for animals, was an amazing gardener and artist. Colourful plants and buzzing insects filled her garden, while inside her home, paintings of the seaside, where she spent her childhood, added a touch of nostalgia. Laura had painted every piece of art in the cottage. She sold some of her artwork in the gift shop in the village. Laura's husband, Peter, was a very important man who worked in the city and wore a navy blue pin-striped suit to work each day. Laura would receive gifts from him whenever he returned from his work trips, and occasionally Sam and Sarah would also receive something. The kids were particularly fond of the koala bear and kangaroo stuffed toys that Peter had brought all the way from Australia.

"We're here to see the adorable golden puppies you have!" Sarah proclaimed with a confident gesture, unveiling her hands in a "Ta Daa!" fashion.

"Well, I have a surprise for you," grinned Laura. "They aren't all golden."

"How can they not all be golden?" asked a slightly confused Sam. "Jess is golden, so they must all be the same as her."

As the children approached the pen and basket that was set up in the dining room, they peered in and sure enough, there they were and among them, one brown bundle of fluff sat proudly with the other four gold fuzzy balls.

"We're as puzzled as you are Sam," Laura winked at Vicky, "This just sometimes happens."

Sarah followed her mother's instructions and threw her shoes against the back door. She climbed in to the pen and sat in the middle of the five cuddly soft friends she was about to make.

"Oh, I love them so much!" she cried, "They are so cuddly." Jess, the mother dog, opened one eye as she lay cosy by the fire, and closed it just as quickly, knowing her babies were safe with these humans. "This is Snowdrop," Sarah continued in a squeaky voice completely different from her normal one, "You must look after her as she is a very special teddy and will keep you safe and warm." The little chocolate dog, from the pile, looked up with her minstrel shaped eyes and licked the soft toy as if to agree with Sarah.

"I like this feeling." thought the pup to herself. "We have a cuddly gift to play with, chew, and toss around. These humans are so kind that they make me feel warm and fuzzy inside."

Sam regretted his decision of not wanting to join his sister in the pen as he watched from afar. It looked such fun in there. "You can come in, Sam," said Sarah, noticing the disappointed look on her brother's face and patting the floor next to her.

"Er...okay I'll come and help you," he replied, secretly pleased at her request.

Vicky and Laura enjoyed their tea and conversation as they dipped ginger biscuits and the children played with the puppies. A couple of minutes later, Sam cut into their discussion, uttering,

"What are you going to do with all these puppies, Laura?"

"There are lots of people who want to buy them," she replied. "In fact, we already have homes for two of the puppies who are going to their new homes in a few weeks."

"So that leaves two who haven't got homes?" a sad Sarah started to say, only to be interrupted by her brother.

"You mean three puppies, Sarah. Two gold and one chocolate brown."

"But the chocolate brown one does have a home," replied his little sister, standing up in the pen, "She's going to be coming to live with us!" Each of the ten little pointed ears belonging to the adorable four-legged friends perked up all at once, and they all turned to look at each other before fixating their eyes on one puppy in particular. Vicky spat out her tea at this declaration from her little girl. "Now remember what Dad said this morning, that ......"

Sarah interrupted her mum to declare, "Cocoa is coming to live with us at Meaburn Hill Farm. Cocoa Pops, to be precise, because I love Cocoa pops for breakfast as they turn all the milk brown and ….."

Sarah's nonstop chatter about dogs, breakfast, and chocolate milk left the two ladies open-mouthed, wondering what Albert's reaction would be. "Oh dear, what on earth will he say?" declared Laura. Sam buried his head in his hands, giggling at his sister's announcement. Yes, he pondered in thought, what is Dad going to say?

Filled with joy, Cocoa barked in agreement with the excited little girl, grateful to be chosen to live with such kind-hearted people. This was a truly joyful day for everyone.

Chapter Three

A New Family

Albert and Vicky had a whirlwind four weeks as they got ready for their new arrival and prepared the farm for autumn and then the winter that would quickly follow. The children, however, did not feel like it went by so quickly. The anticipation of welcoming a new addition to their family filled them with excitement, prompting them to visit her multiple times and develop a close connection with their new puppy. Anna's attempt to persuade her mum to adopt the other gold puppy had ended in failure, much to the disappointment of the little girl. Will she ever have the chance to own a real dog? Sarah and Emily comforted Anna by assuring her that she could play with their dogs anytime she wished, with the intention of making her feel better. So, this puppy for sale went through training to assist individuals who have trouble hearing. How amazing, a dog specifically trained to help with hearing.

Laura and Peter decided to keep the final golden labrador puppy, which made Jess, the mother dog, very happy. His name was Oli and was Cocoa's best friend… so Sarah said. "Everybody needs a best friend. Whether you're a dog or a human". Wise words from such a tiny person.

It was a challenge to persuade Albert that getting a new puppy was a good idea. "Who is going to walk and feed her? Haven't we enough to do without a new family member?" he'd grumbled daily. However, after a few promises from Vicky that she would take charge and from Sam that he would take the new family member for walks - oh and a few desperate tears from Sarah, who didn't promise to do much other than cuddle her new puppy - it was agreed, Cocoa would come to live at Meaburn Hill Farm. Vicky was quietly excited about the new arrival too, but, of course, stood by her husband's firm rules on where the puppy would sleep and eat... for now!

"Cocoa is not allowed to jump on or sleep on the sofa and will be confined to the kitchen. She must lie on her blanket when she comes into the lounge and will not be allowed in the dining room while we are eating. Oh, and she is definitely not allowed in the bedrooms. Is this all clear?"

"Yes, Daddy. Of course," parroted the children glancing sideways at each other, wondering if setting up that blanket in Sam's bedroom was a good idea after all.

After what felt like forever, Saturday morning finally arrived. Today was the day made even more exciting by the sun streaming through the windows. Cocoa was being picked up that morning from the Carr's house. A brand new soft bed in maroon and cream, along with a shiny bowl and a pink bone-shaped rubber toy, has been set up in the kitchen by the oven. The house was full of giddiness and noise, not helped by Sarah running around the lounge barking and yelping like a dog. Sam was clinging on to the new lead and collar that had been bought that morning in the village. He had been down to the pet shop with his dad to choose the colour of Cocoa's new collar. "It just has to be red, Dad. Red is such a cool colour and my first car is going to be red," he'd exclaimed. It was also the team colour of their favourite football team.

"Red it is!" said Albert as he put a ten pound note down on the counter. He was getting quite excited himself now that the new puppy was arriving, but he would never tell his wife or the children that.

"Are we all ready to go and collect our new family member?" shouted Vicky from the garden, pulling out weeds as she waited. Vicky would never leave a weed unpulled if she spotted it.

"Yes!" screamed Sarah, running out of the kitchen, tripping over the step and stumbling into a run as she pretended to bark.

"I'm coming too - wait for me!" shouted Sam. "I've got her collar and lead here." Albert followed on slowly as he locked the back door. "No turning back now," he sighed, looking back at the lovely tidy kitchen. Little did he know that wouldn't last!

Within what seemed an entire hour to the children, but was in fact only minutes, the Cooper family arrived at the Carrs' Cottage. They stepped out of the vehicle and made their way excitedly to the back entrance. Sam knocked quietly on the door so as not to frighten the so very much wanted puppy inside. "Will Jess be sad to say goodbye to Cocoa?" asked a teary-eyed Sarah as they waited patiently for the door to open.

"I'm sure she will miss her," replied her mum, "but she will see her lots as we will go for walks with Laura, Jess and her puppy Oli."

"I hope this collar fits her," said Sam, still waiting anxiously for the door to open.

"Hello!" A cheery Laura appeared at the open window upstairs. "The door is open - just come inside." Laura was always smiley and happy. She would be a great mum, Vicky thought to herself. Maybe one day she will have some children of her own.

In the lounge, there she stood. Cocoa, the chocolate Labrador, wagging her tail happily with her back to the family of four. Hearing the door click shut, Cocoa quickly spun around, causing her to stumble and making the children laugh. Just like that, she quickly got up and bounded towards them. As a ball of energy and chaos approached, Sam leapt on to the sofa and watched as she knocked over the standing lamp in the corner of the room. "Here we go," sighed Laura. "Chaos Cocoa. She's clearly very excited to see you all: her new family." Albert looked on, thinking to himself – What on earth have I done?

Jess, the mummy dog, grunted and just lay down as if to disapprove of her puppy. Instead of calming Cocoa down, Vicky and Sarah's laughter and shrieks made her even more wild and giddy. Without wasting any time, Cocoa hurriedly made her way back to them, snatching Snowdrop the teddy from the basket along the way. She had developed a close attachment to Sarah's favourite toy, which now had a missing ear and eye. Sam stayed firmly on the sofa; mouth wide open.

"I have your bunny rabbit right here. I did a great job of taking care of it for you. Will I have more toys waiting for me in my new home?" Cocoa jumped up at Sarah, nuzzling the ragged remains of the soft toy into her arms. As the puppy had grown bigger over the past few weeks, its excitement had grown too, resulting in louder and louder barking.

"Sit!" commanded Laura in a quiet but firm voice. "Oh my goodness Cocoa, your new family won't want to take you home if you carry on behaving like this." Laura winked at Sarah, assuring her that her new cuddly pal would still be going with her that day. At this point, the rest of the family weren't too sure! Cocoa rolled over instead of sitting. "She hasn't quite grasped the *sit* command yet I see." declared Sam still clinging to the mint green cushion he was using as a shield.

“I can’t wait to tell Anna and Emily about our new puppy,” smiled Sarah. Anna, still desperate for a puppy of her own, still hadn't yet been successful in persuading her parents. “They’re both going to love Cocoa!”

"Alright, guys, there's no turning back from here! I'm coming home with you."

With that, Cocoa confidently made her way to the door, securely clipped to the lead, pulling Sam behind. Vicky and Albert exchanged quick glances, uncertain about how they would handle this new family member. Too late to change their minds now!

Chapter Four

Home Sweet Home

With a few helpful tips from Laura, Cocoa was ready to start her new life at Meaburn Hill Farm. With her tongue hanging out, panting hard, she proudly sat on Sarah's knee, staring out of the half open car window. As they drove, her ears fluttered and flapped in the wind, while her nose twitched at every scent that came her way.

Despite Sam's kind gesture of letting his sister have the first chance to hold their new puppy, he secretly had doubts about this lively chocolate puff-ball that was about to join their home. She was quite unpredictable!

"Can we take Cocoa to church tomorrow, Mummy?" Sarah piped up from the back seat.

"Absolutely not!" glared Albert through the rear-view mirror of the car before his wife had a chance to speak. Sarah kept nuzzling and gently stroking Cocoa's ears, whispering words of love and savouring the scent of a new puppy. Cocoa groaned happily, enjoying this new attention, while Sam observed, hoping that his turn to hold her would come soon as the puppy had settled down a bit after leaving Laura's cottage.

As the car neared the house, it gently rolled over the speed bumps on the road. Soon the car had come to a standstill. They were home. While the others went to the back of the car to open the boot for Cocoa to jump down, Albert pulled the handbrake into position. Cocoa had a good sniff around the orchard and the vegetable patch at the side of the house, wondering where would be best to do her 'business'. Cocoa thought there were many delightful things to see and play with here, like a chewable sweeping brush, a hosepipe for creating numerous holes, and a swimming pond. "This place was just the ticket!" Cocoa mused and bounced around for a while. The family squealed in delight, watching their new family member play and dart amongst the trees. Picking up the odd apple off the ground and devouring it quicker than you could say the word 'apple', Cocoa continued to make the family very happy and amused. Who knew dogs liked to eat apples?

After entering the house, Cocoa seemed to relax, breathing heavily from her wild sprint and investigating the kitchen with her sense of smell. Making a loud slurping noise as she finished the bowl of fresh water, Cocoa shook her head and splattered drool all over the room. She appeared to enjoy her new bed beside the cosy oven. Sam sat with her in the dog bed, petting her and getting acquainted with his new companion. After her thrilling day, Cocoa was exhausted and drifted into a deep sleep, snoring loudly. "Ah, this is not too bad after all," said a proud Albert. "I think Cocoa is going to fit in with us all just fine."

Vicky pottered round the kitchen, keeping a watchful eye on her new kitchen buddy. Tonight's meal was a homemade vegetable lasagne and salad. The aroma of the cooking supper caused Cocoa's nose to twitch while she slept. Her food obsession was clear as she dreamt of a bowl overflowing with lasagne and dog biscuits, dismissing the idea of salad altogether. With a sense of pride for her new puppy and the apparent simplicity of this settling in task, Vicky entered the dining room where the rest were waiting for dinner. "The lasagne is ready," she announced. "It's just on the sideboard cooling, so shall we start with our prayer of thanks for our food and our new guest? Albert darling?"

Albert began his prayer, "Oh yes, um... Dear Lord, we are grateful for our new family member, Cocoa, who joined us today, and for the food we are about to..." CRASH! There was a loud commotion coming from the kitchen. The four of them lifted their heads from prayer, stared at each other, and quickly rushed into the kitchen where the noise was. To everyone's surprise and dismay, there on the sideboard - yes, actually standing on the sideboard! - was Cocoa.

"Oh no, my blessed lasagne!" cried Vicky. As sure as lemons are yellow, there she was, with her head down, tail batting furiously side to side and fluffy bottom in the air. In the limited time she had, Cocoa greedily consumed as much lasagne as possible before being abruptly removed from the unit like a sack of potatoes. After being thrown back into her bed, Cocoa licked her lips and let out an almighty burp. Sam and Sarah watched, unsure if they should burst into laughter or tears, knowing there would be no homemade lasagne for dinner. On second thoughts, it was probably not a good idea to laugh by the maddening look on Dad's face.

Albert stood, quite still in shock, not quite believing what he'd seen. "How did she get up on the sideboard?"

Cocoa watched on, thinking, "Easy peasy, just check everyone is distracted, nudge the stool into position with my wet nose and jump. After three attempts, it's quite simple then to balance in just the right way so as not to fall off."

"What a naughty puppy!" Albert raised his voice and shook his finger sharply at Cocoa, who just tilted her head and then settled back down.

"Mmmmm, these humans are so bossy. What's all the fuss about? They've a lot to learn about pups," Cocoa murmured to herself, not in the slightest bit upset by being in big trouble on her first night. Vicky dashed over to grab the remains of the lasagne from the floor, shouting orders about what to do next to the rest of the family as she cleaned.

After mopping away every last bit of lasagne and having a fish and chip supper from the local chip shop, the Cooper family went to bed after a chaotic first day. Right before switching off his bedroom light, Sam made the decision to pen an exhilarating retelling of the day in his diary, making sure to embellish what had truly occurred. Sarah drifted off to sleep, imagining her new cuddly friend and planning which princess outfits she would put on her new puppy the next day. She felt fuzzy and warm inside, loving the new family member unconditionally.

"We've moved all the food, haven't we? There is nothing else she can possibly eat, right?" asked Vicky as she got in to bed and turned to her husband with tired eyes. Today had worn her out!

"I can't see what else could happen," he replied, "Cocoa was clearly just very nervous and over excited on her first day with us and doesn't know the rules yet." Albert felt a pang of guilt at how he'd raised his voice earlier in front of the children.

Both adults, completely worn out, decided to turn off the lights and get some sleep.

Meanwhile, downstairs, a cheeky and mischievous 8-week-old Cocoa had other ideas. "That lady they call mummy seems nice," she thought to herself, "The daddy man seems a bit grumpy, but I'm sure I'll be able to get on his good side. The brother and sister are going to be such fun, especially playing in the muddy puddles. Now where did they say the doggy toilet was...?"

Uh Oh. Splat ......

Chapter Five

Messy Morning

The sun peeped through the curtains into the bedroom, waking up a sleepy Sam with a gentle nudge. Last night had been fun, even though Mum and Dad hadn't seen the funny side. Maybe he would be braver today and get to know Cocoa a little better, providing she didn't bound towards him again. "Yes," he said to himself out loud, "I'll go downstairs now before the others are awake and say hello to our new pup and get her breakfast ready."

Sam pushed his favourite blue and red rocket patterned blanket aside and got out of bed, stretching and yawning silently. He put on his new slippers from Grandma and reached for his old red dressing gown hanging on the back of the door. "I really need a new one of these," he pondered, "three buttons are now missing on this one". With this, he crept down the creaky staircase, fastening the belt on his dressing gown as he went, not wanting to wake the others. If Sarah heard him, she'd just want to come and take over. He cautiously opened the door, ensuring it didn't squeak, and entered the dimly lit kitchen where all the curtains were tightly closed, preventing the sun from shining through. Holding his breath, he prayed that Cocoa wouldn't pounce on him. To his astonishment, she was seated in the centre of the kitchen floor, looking incredibly adorable and behaving perfectly.

"Aw, you good girl," he whispered, "You have been such a good girl overnight." He made his way towards her and then... Squelch!

There it was. New slippers foot printed into a brown pile of... well, you know what! "What on earth?" cried Sam, not really knowing where to step now.

It was clear that moving towards the sink full of last night's dishes and the light switch was the wrong choice. As if things couldn't get any worse, Sam's left foot sank into a warm, wet puddle on the kitchen floor.

Cocoa just stayed sat, wet tail swishing side to side, staring at him, thinking, "How silly not to put my training mat down before bed. What do they expect? I'm far too young to wait all night to do my doo doo's. The brother seems kind though, so I'll go and say good morning." With this, Cocoa bounded over to Sam, sliding as she hit the wet pool on the floor, and continued to jump up, soggy paws placed perfectly on his pyjama bottoms and the bottom of his already scruffy dressing gown. "Oh, great!" Sam huffed in dismay.

The kitchen lights were switched on, causing Sam great embarrassment as Mum, Dad, and Sarah appeared at the door to investigate the commotion. They'd heard sounds of distress and words like, "Oh no Cocoa!" and, "Get off, you silly dog!" from upstairs and had come down in a hurry to investigate. And there they were, Cocoa and Sam, both wet and dirty from the several puddles scattered around the kitchen floor, amongst other things.

"Awwww, Saaaaam!" Sarah whined in an accusing voice, giggling underneath her breath at the mess before her eyes. She did like to tease her brother an awful lot.

"What?" Sam shot a glance in his sister's direction, looking very annoyed and flushed. "I didn't cause all this mess. I came down to try to help by feeding this ridiculously wild animal."

"Ok everybody, calm down," said Vicky, pulling at each side of her straggly morning hair. "We need to start cleaning up this mess. Albert, go and get the lead please and take this crazy beast outside while I clean up. Sam go upstairs and get out of those messy pyjamas and dressing gown. Leave your dirty slippers there. Why do you still wear that tatty old thing, anyway? You need a new one."

Sam stormed off, grumbling to himself and muttering, "Yes, I do need a new one, mother. Especially now!"

Albert, unhappy about being assigned the task of taking Cocoa out in the cold in yesterday's clothes that he'd grabbed from the bedroom floor, decided it was best not to mention this to his wife. She was already in a bad mood from the night before, as well as what they had now woken up to.

"Come on, Cocoa," Albert groaned, grabbing a towel to at least try to dry cocoa off a bit from the dramatic wet skid she had made across the floor.

"I'm coming Daddy," shouted Sarah, "I'll just go and get Cocoa an outfit from the dress-up box and we can take her down the lane."

"Oh, even better," grunted Albert under his breath, "One chaotic dog and one crazy daughter," but he knew that once Sarah had an idea in her head to do something, it was easier to just go along with it than try to change her mind. Especially where dressing up and imagination were concerned.

The presence of their new companion and the bite of the cold air on their cheeks brought a sense of calm to the pair as they strolled along the lane. In a gentle gesture, Sarah's small, pink, nail-polished hand intertwined with her dad's larger, weathered hand from the farm. With a beaming smile, she thanked her dad for giving them permission to bring Cocoa to live with them. "Thank you for letting Cocoa come and live with us Daddy, I do love her sooooo much! She will not only be a great friend to all of us, but so much more." This melted Albert's heart and all the frustration he'd felt from the earlier antics drifted away. It was funny how Vicky, Sam and Sarah managed to get their own way around him, but after all, the only thing he ever desired was the best for his family and their happiness. Cocoa pulled ahead on the lead, fully dressed in a tutu and tiara from the dress-up box, looking around at the two humans in approval, as if she understood everything Sarah was saying. And you know what... she did!

The time passed quickly as Sarah chatted and made up stories for an hour, and now they were all back at the farmhouse, including Cocoa. Sam signalled through the window to the travellers that it was safe, then opened the kitchen door for them to enter. Not only was the floor clean, but Mum had also calmed down and was preparing bacon butties for everyone. An unfamiliar smell caused Cocoa's nose to twitch in curiosity. "I wonder if I'll get to try?" she thought to herself, tongue hanging out.

"Don't you be thinking you're getting a treat after your behaviour, Cocoa Pops," announced Vicky.

Cocoa lay down on the floor, grunting as she dropped in a heap at the sheer disappointment. "There's my answer... grrrrrr."

"Don't worry, Cocoa," whispered Sam as he bent down and patted the brown velvet head below. "I'll save you some of my bacon." Cocoa's sad-looking chocolate button eyes were very hard to ignore and certainly seemed to help her get her own way. She was learning very quickly how to get around this family. Day two was going very well.

Chapter Six

Sunday Lunch

The household had all calmed down and everyone had enjoyed their bacon butties, including Cocoa's secret portion. With bits of crust left on the plates, it was now time for Vicky, Albert, and the two children to go to church. Sunday was always a busy day for the family, as they would usually invite somebody home for lunch after the morning service. Everybody in the village knew of Vicky's famous homemade apple and rhubarb crumble, made with the deliciously juicy apples from their orchard. There was usually a choice of fresh cream, hot, scrummy custard or yellow soft ice cream, however, today there was only custard. Things had been a little busy with Cocoa's arrival, so not much shopping had been done.

"Mummy, please can we each invite one of our friends for lunch today to come and meet our new puppy?" asked Sarah as they bundled into the car, very last minute it has to be said.

"Oh yes, can we?" echoed Sam. Sarah was much better at getting her own way, he thought to himself and used this to get what he wanted too.

"Well, I had thought of asking the vicar and his wife today, but I guess I can squeeze two extra around the table."

"Yes, yes, thank you!" they both shouted, and started to discuss which friends to invite, not hearing their dad repeatedly asking them to put their seatbelts on.

"Seatbelts!" he yelled for the fifth time.

At last, they were on their way, and Cocoa, who wasn't supposed to be there, observed them from the dining-room windowsill. She had quickly mastered the art of opening the door connecting the two rooms. "Push down the handle while head-butting the door by jumping. Yes, I'm in!"

The car disappeared, prompting her to jump down and accidentally knock over the pale cream porcelain vase that Albert had bought as a birthday gift for his wife. Sniffing the pink fallen flowers that had sat proudly in it, Cocoa seemed disappointed that they weren't food. "I'll have a taste anyway, just in case. Yuck."

As she spat out the remains of the rose head she had just devoured, she thought to herself about the horrible and perfumy taste of those things, which led to a dramatic sneeze.

Meanwhile, down in the village, an hour had now passed and church was coming to an end for another week. This week's lesson had been about God's creatures and how precious they are and should be looked after. This was a very good lesson for Sam and Sarah on the weekend they had got their new puppy. The final hymn was 'All things bright and beautiful', both children giggling as they changed the words of 'all creatures great and small' to 'all dogs, great and small'.

Sam's friend, Ben, who he had wanted to invite, was missing from church as he had caught chicken pox. "How annoying!" he moaned to himself as Sarah waltzed past him with her friend Anna, both barking and jumping up at everybody. Anna was desperate to meet Cocoa – to have a Border Collie was her dream. She was very excited to be chosen as Cocoa's first guest. "Great, these two are going to be so annoying, Dad," Sam continued in a whiney voice.

Albert gave Sam a little play punch on the arm and said, "You can help me build the kennel outside after lunch. We'll leave the giggly girls to it." Sam, now beaming, was pleased with this idea. Who wants to play dogs? It's much more fun building a kennel with Dad - how grown up!

"We'll see you back at the farmhouse," shouted Vicky to Reverend Tom and his wife, Jane. "The kettle will be on."

Albert, Vicky and the children all walked down the lane to the car which was parked outside the Vicarage. "The lunch will be just about ready by the time we get home," said Vicky as the car wound down country lanes to the Farmhouse which was a ten-minute drive away.

"Are we having Yorkshire puddings?" shouted Anna. "They're my favourite!"

"Yes, Yorkshire puddings, but you must eat all your vegetables too." Vicky turned round to reply.

"Sounds just like my mum," whispered Anna to Sam, who was sitting in the middle of the two girls.

"That's mums for you," he replied with a smirk.

"I just cannot wait to show you our perfect puppy, Anna. I've invited Emily too, seeing as Ben can't come." Sarah sniggered and leaned closer to Sam teasingly, causing him to roll his eyes in frustration. He knew that the rest of the afternoon would be filled with laughter and shrieks. "In fact, Emily's been poorly a lot recently so she can only come for a little while as she has to rest," said Sarah thoughtfully. Then, with a big smile breaking across her face, "Cocoa's so shiny and bouncy."

"Too bouncy," mumbled Sam.

The family arrived home to Cocoa, bouncing at them as they walked through the stable door to the kitchen. Emily arrived at the same time, just as they got home.

"Wow! She is a giddy pup, Sarah!" laughed Emily, "Come on, let's go inside and I'll show you two how to train her!" Emily walked proudly ahead with Sarah and Anna following in awe of their friend's wisdom on dogs, especially having three dogs of her own. Sam looked up, noticing the door to the dining room was open.

"Er, how did Cocoa get through there? Why is there a vase on the floor? Mum, your flowers are a bit chewed, I think?" So many sentences were coming out of Sam's mouth it was hard to take it all in. The three girls shrieked as Cocoa bounded towards them, jumping and licking their faces.

"I told you she was bouncy!" giggled Sarah, as Anna looked on in shock at the complete chaos around her. "Cocoa, get down!" In a frenzy, the wild puppy snatched Anna's scarf and bolted to the next room, prompting them both to yell in alarm. Emily shouted instructions, knowing all about dogs, but this time, it wasn't working. Without any delay, Cocoa rushed back to the family, holding the scarf and two rose heads in her mouth. More screams could be heard from the girls, accompanied by an "Oh my!" from Albert, as he tried to catch the crazy brown bundle before him. Sam had, by this time, shut himself out on the other side of the stable door to protect himself from the beast inside.

"Tom and Jane will be here any minute!" shouted Vicky in despair, with her hands up to her burning cheeks, "What on earth are we going to do?" As quick as she had said the words, there they were, stood on the other side of the back door with Sam, looking on in amazement at the chaos before them. Just as Albert was about to apologise, Jane started to giggle, then Tom started to laugh, the young girls joining in. "Welcome to the chaotic world of Cocoa!" Sam looked pleased with his announcement, which made everybody laugh again. Who would have thought such a small puppy could cause so much mayhem?

Soon enough, the half-eaten flowers, the vase and the water were all cleaned up and Sam was enjoying a game of chess with Reverend Tom while waiting for lunch.

Vicky and Jane chatted away in the kitchen and Cocoa lay in her bed as if nothing had happened... this time in a mermaid outfit. Sarah, Emily and Anna were playing upstairs whilst coming up with ideas of how they could persuade Anna's mum to get a dog.

"Will you be back at school with us next week, Emily?" Anna asked as she sat the toy dogs from the toy box in a row in size order.

"I really hope so Anna, I am getting rather bored with being at home. I bet school isn't half as fun without me there, is it?" Emily laughed cheekily at her own bold statement.

Sarah hugged her friend and admired how she always saw the bright side of every situation.

Albert had taken himself off into the garden, pretending to look for wood to make the kennel, but actually for a much-needed minute to himself. He smiled as he thought about the family and friends inside the house. How he loved them so much! Even Cocoa... just a bit.

Chapter Seven

Walk in the Woods

Autumn had well and truly arrived, marking the passing of nine weeks of school. The velvety green foliage had changed into shades of russet red and brown, gently cascading from the trees. It was the half-term holiday for Sam and Sarah.

"Yes! No school for a week. What are we doing today?" shouted an excited Sarah from upstairs as she pulled on her pink leggings and yellow jumper. Sam looked on as he passed her bedroom door, thinking about how his sister's outfit didn't match at all. "Hey Sam, don't I look so pretty in this outfit?" she beamed, "My two favourite colours. I'm going to ask mummy to put a purple ribbon in my hair too."

"Er yeah... er I don't know," he replied, rushing awkwardly towards the stairs to run down and get his breakfast.

Cocoa had been out for her first walk of the day to try to get rid of some of her energy and calm her down.

"Today, we are going to go for a walk into the woods, gang," declared Albert. "It is going to be Cocoa's first time off the lead." Cocoa lifted her head from the floor, feeling excited.

"Two walks! This is going to be a fun day. Going off lead, I wonder what mischief I can get up to?" she mused.

Joining the rest of the family, Sarah swiped Sam's meticulously buttered toast from the table.

"Hey!" he shouted, "that's mine."

"It isn't now," she giggled, taking a huge bite from the buttery toast.

"Mum, tell her..." Sam drew the line at his food being taken.

"Now, now, you two, enough bickering. We need to eat up, do our school diary homework, and then we can get going into the woods to enjoy the rest of the day."

"Homework?" both children moaned at the same time. "But I really don't know what to write about," Sam continued in a moaning voice. "Neither do I!" shouted Sarah, folding her arms and pushing out her bottom lip.

"Well, you can write about what we are doing today," said Vicky whilst wiping off the blob of jam that had dropped on to the table. Cocoa lay under the table, licking her lips and catching any bit of food that might fall. "Shame the jam didn't come my way," she thought as she rolled her eyes and settled back down in the hope of at least something edible coming her way.

"Okay, well how about we do the diary homework when we get back then as we will have more to write about?" suggested Sam, raising his eyebrows in question as he spoke.

"Yes, can we please?" echoed Sarah.

"Okay, you two, go and get your wellies and coats on." Albert suggested collecting leaves to stick into the children's school books while they were out. Both children quickly cleared the table and ran out of the room before Albert could change his mind. Sarah hugged her brother tightly to show her appreciation for his idea. "Uh sisters!" groaned Sam, but he was secretly feeling proud of his idea and the fact it was impressing his sister. The two children had a strong bond, as both siblings and close friends.

Thirty minutes later, the family was bundled up in bobble hats and scarves, trudging through the muddy woods in their wellies. Cocoa was still secure on her lead, at least for now, despite the fact that Albert was being dragged along.

"Hey, there's Emily!" Sarah ran excitedly towards her friend who she hadn't seen last week as she had been poorly again and missing from class. Emily was walking with a limp, with her mum Martha, and their three dogs, Scout, Digby, and Amber.

"I missed you sooooo much at school!" said Sarah in a loving voice. "It's just not the same when you're not there."

Emily smiled for a second, and then her smile quickly disappeared. "I haven't been very well at all," declared Emily. "My leg gets so sore when I walk. I might have sprained it or something. Or maybe my leg is going to fall off. Or maybe even worse ... someone will have to chop it off." Emily giggled at her own dramatic declaration and description of her sore leg. She did like to shock people with her statements.

Sarah looked on with worry. "Oh my gosh, Emily! Don't say that. I really hope it's soon better than we can walk our dogs together. I've been desperate to walk with you since Cocoa arrived." The two girls hugged and squeezed as if their lives depended on it. This really was a friendship that was going to last forever and ever.

"Maybe you could come over for tea later on in the week while it's the school holidays?" enquired Emily, "And sleep over if you want to? My mum is rubbish at cooking, but Dad makes a brilliant mascarpone pasta and veg thingy-me-bob."

"I'd love to come. We could carry on making up our songs and dances," Sarah replied, feeling thrilled that she was going to get some special time with her sister-like friend.

While the girls chatted and made plans, they noticed the Mum's looked very serious and deep in conversation. "Grown-ups are so serious, aren't they?" declared Emily. "Sarah, I hope we never lose our sense of fun and adventure as we get older." Holding each other's hands tightly, their grip drained the colour, turning their hands into a pale white.

"We'll be silly forever." shouted Sarah loudly, both Mums now turning around to see what the commotion was all about.

Further behind, still making their way up the muddy track, were the boys with a panting pulling Cocoa.

"When can we let her run, Dad?" said Sam, collecting conkers and stuffing them into his coat pocket as he walked. Sarah and Vicky were now strolling ahead alone, making up stories of the fairies and witches who lived in the woods.

"Well, I did have a practice letting her off the lead on her morning walk and she did very well at coming back to her name being shouted, so shall we try now?" smiled Albert.

"Yes, yes!" shouted Sam in excitement. "Can I do it?" he continued, unclipping the lead from her collar, "Ready, Steady, ..."

"This is going to be great! Yippee!" thought Cocoa as she started to bubble inside with excitement. "I need to run fast to see if I can catch up to Emily and Scout. He's my bestest friend and I haven't seen him for ages and ages." Before Sam had finished his sentence, she shot off ahead like a sports car towards Vicky and Sarah, both of them still in a world of their own making up stories.

"Mum, watch out!" shouted Sam, cupping his hands around his mouth so his statement carried across the woods, "Cocoa is on her way." No sooner had he shouted, Cocoa ran between the story daydreamers, knocking Sarah off her feet, who landed in the wet leaves, pink leggings now covered in mud.

“Cocoa, come back!” yelled Albert, hoping that the practice with her this morning hadn’t been a one-off successful event. “Come back here now!” he continued to shout. Cocoa was already disappearing into the trees up ahead. “Dad, oh no! What are we going to do?” Sam was now trying to hold back the tears, feeling like it was his fault this had happened. “What if I have lost our dog?”

“Calm down, son. It isn’t your fault. We’ll find her. She’ll come back in a minute, you watch."

Albert and Sam caught up to a shocked Vicky and a flushed Sarah. “That dog is just crazy!” exclaimed Vicky as she brushed as much mud as she could from Sarah’s leggings. “How are we ever going to find her now?” With this, both children began to cry.

Vicky's tone changed to a calmer, more endearing one. "Come on now, don't cry. Cocoa will soon come back when she's hungry." Albert looked at Vicky with a look that whispered, I'm not sure how we're going to solve this.

Even after an hour, there was still no sign of Cocoa. Both children were extremely upset as they searched for hidden paths and yelled loudly. It was getting cold and starting to rain. "Cocoa is going to be wet and sad," sobbed Sarah. "She will be wondering where we are."

"I think you should take the children back to the house and I will carry on looking for Cocoa," announced Albert.

"Okay, but I really can't think where she would have got to? I hope we find her soon." Vicky took the hands of both children and started to head back home.

"I should never have taken the lead off," said a very sad and tearful Sam, "She just got too excited when I shouted ready, steady, go." He wiped his tear-stained face with muddy hands. The half-hour walk back to the house felt like a lifetime to the three sad family members, all thinking about where Cocoa could be. Sam dragged his feet through the muddy leaves, making a path and hoping that Cocoa would pick up on this scent and follow it home. He was a real thinker and was already working out a plan as they walked about how he would find her. Sarah just sobbed and sobbed.

The incline of the hill leading to the family farmhouse seemed much steeper than usual. All of a sudden, Jessie emerged from the house across the lane from theirs, standing at the top. Urgently waving her arms, she called out, "Vicky, Vicky, come quickly!"

Vicky picked up her pace, dragging a soaked and sobbing Sarah behind her. Sam overtook his mum and started to march quickly up the hill, as a wave of relief washed over him, towards Jessie.

"What is it, Miss Jessie?" he shouted to the old lady, still waving her arms. Jessie was a very special lady to the family. Each time Vicky needed to run errands, she'd leave the children with Jessie, who would slyly give them some pennies to buy toffees.

"Come quickly. I think your puppy is in the middle of the lane!" With this, all three of them started to run up the hill. As they reached the top, there she was, just as Jessie had said, sat in the middle of the lane, eating a shortbread biscuit that Jessie had given her to keep her there, being stroked by John, her husband. All the tractors and cars were stopped around her, not able to get past until Cocoa had decided to lick every crumb from the road. Farmer Mick, from the next village, didn't look too pleased to be held up by this nonsense, with his sheep *baaaing* loudly from the trailer behind his tractor.

Sarah went from sobbing to tears of joy, while Sam hastily wiped his face with muddy hands to hide his own tears. Even though he thought this was a good enough reason for crying.

"You are a naughty puppy!" shouted Vicky as she put the little brown fluff-ball back on the lead.

"What's all the fuss about? The disappointment is all mine, having run all that way and not finding my pal, Scout. He must've headed a different way home," pondered a very hungry Cocoa, sniffing for every last crumb of biscuit between the gravel.

Just as Vicky was finishing scolding Cocoa, Albert arrived behind them.

“Oh, thank goodness!” he puffed, feeling quite out of breath from running around the woods, “I was so worried about you, our little gorgeous bundle of fun.” Vicky began to grin as her husband stroked and fussed over her – all the anger and upset went away and the whole family knelt down to cuddle their chocolate friend.

“Why am I getting so many cuddles?” thought Cocoa to herself, still reaching for the very last crumb. “I don’t usually get cuddled for eating biscuits and running into the road. I must do this more often.” Her tail was now batting side to side in a frenzy of love and excitement.

“Let’s go home and have a nice cup of hot chocolate,” said Vicky.

"Hot chocolate?" Cocoa's ears pricked up in confusion. "I hope they're not going to put me in a pan, cook and eat me."

“Well, I certainly have a lot to write in my school diary now after the day we’ve just had,” said Sam with a half giggle, still feeling shaken by the day's events.

"We certainly do," agreed Sarah. "Can you help me with mine, Sam?".

"Okay," he agreed, taking his little sister's hand as they walked home. Even though brother and sister, this really was another friendship that was going to last forever.

Chapter Eight

It's Christmas

After living with the family for three months, Cocoa was beginning to get a better handle on the rules. Well, a tiny bit more. Although she now walked calmly beside Albert, she occasionally would sprint towards dropped food or shiny wrappers, causing him to almost lose his grip. Unless there was a stray sausage roll from someone's picnic, she would always return obediently when released from the lead in the woods. There was no doubt: Food was what Cocoa loved the most.

The Meaburn Hill farmhouse was buzzing with excitement. Because it was Christmas Eve, Grandma and Grandpa were coming to stay for a few days.

"Father Christmas should be en route to our house by now, Mum," Sam stated, as he enjoyed calculating Santa's whereabouts. "Since it's eleven in the morning here, he must be heading towards Australia."

"Yes, I suppose he will be," she replied, feeling just as excited as the children. This was her favourite time of the year.

Albert had been working on the farm since 5 a.m., and now he was done for the day. He anticipated a peaceful afternoon with his family, relieved that all the work was finished for the day. Both he and Vicky loved to cook and entertain. Albert was excitedly looking forward to the Christmas lunch that would be on the table the next day. The room filling with the scent of Christmas, making everyone's mouths water in delight. Christmas was such a special time, made extra special this year by Cocoa being part of the family.

Back in the house, Sarah was sitting at the kitchen table making Christmas decorations out of coloured paper and several other craft items to hang around the house.

"Not too much glitter, Sarah, we don't want it everywhere!" shouted Vicky from the dining room. She was always proud of how her dining room table looked at Christmas. The place mats proudly displayed reindeer pictures, alongside co-ordinating napkins and tablecloth. It seemed like tomorrow would be a great day. As always, Cocoa was under the table at Sarah's feet, enjoying the aroma of the food cooking in the oven ready for their Christmas eve supper. In her sleep, she imagined a bountiful plate of food and questioned whether she would be able to taste it. Her nose twitching as she slept. Everything was peaceful and organised in the house, getting it ready for the arrival of Father Christmas and, of course, the grandparents. Covered in bright lights and shiny baubles gathered over the years from family vacations, the Christmas tree stood proudly in the sitting-room window. Just at that minute... ding dong! The doorbell chimed loudly through the house. With a sudden bang, Cocoa hit her head under the table, making glittery pots fly and barking loudly while running between the kitchen and the lounge.

“Calm down, Cocoa!” they all shouted at once. “It’s just Grandma and Grandpa.” Vicky opened the front door to welcome her parents with Sam and Sarah not far behind and, of course, ... Cocoa.

“Shut the kitchen door and keep Cocoa in there!” shouted Vicky, as Cocoa bounced toward them. Sarah quickly did as she was asked, just in time, hearing a thud as Cocoa slammed in to the closed door – phew! Grandma and Grandpa were safe, for now anyway. They stood looking at the tall, beautifully dressed tree for at least ten minutes, ooh-ing and ahh-ing at each bauble that they had seen at least five times before.

"Can we let Cocoa in to the sitting room now, Mummy?" said Sarah, still holding the door shut.

"Yes, okay. Brace yourselves," Vicky replied, rolling her eyes.

Nobody was prepared for what was to come. From the kitchen ran a sticky, glittered creature, bouncing with glee.

"My decorations!" shouted an alarmed Sarah. "She's been chewing my homemade decorations."

Cocoa bounded up to Grandma and Grandpa, with sticky paws and glittery tail wagging.

"What is all this mess?" A voice came from behind them. Albert was standing at the back door.

At the sound of his voice, Cocoa spun around in excitement, nearly toppling the Christmas tree, luckily saved by Grandpa. Cocoa sprinted through the dining room, just about avoiding the table and leaping over the chair, before enthusiastically greeting him with her sticky paws. Her tail was now also completely covered in the glue and glitter that had scattered all over the kitchen floor.

"Christmas is fun," thought Cocoa to herself, "Especially the sticky and shiny things stuck to my fur. And Grandma and Grandpa are here ... just to see me."

"Oh my!" exclaimed Grandma Dorothy. "She certainly is as wild as you said."

"She's really excited to see you both, that's for sure," added Sam.

A few minutes of to-ing and fro-ing from room to room, bottom tucked under for maximum speed, and Cocoa began to slow. Phew! "I don't think she realises how big she is," said Vicky. "she just ploughs through everything as if she is still a little puppy, but she's grown so much."

"How rude!" thought Cocoa to herself, "Making comments on my size. I don't comment on Mother's size."

"Let's get that kettle on. Mince pie anyone?" asked an exhausted Vicky, clipping her straggly hair back into a ponytail to relieve some of the heat.

"Yes please," came an echo around the room of hungry voices and a woof from Cocoa.

"I think Cocoa is saying yes please too," laughed Sam, "None for you girl, I'm afraid." Cocoa groaned in response, knowing exactly what was being said.

All was now calm once again in the Farmhouse and Christmas Eve night was drawing in.

"I hope Father Christmas brings me what I have wished for," exclaimed Sarah, cheeks flushed from sitting too near the open fire toasting her marshmallows.

"And what might that be?" asked her dad, lifting her away from the glow of the flames as they grappled.

"A friend for Cocoa," she announced and the whole family shouted, "Oh no!" rolling their eyes at the same time.

"I wonder if Father Christmas has received my letter that I secretly posted a few weeks ago?" Sarah mused to herself. Cocoa slowly lifted one eyelid as she listened to the conversation, then drifted off, dreaming of mince pies and presents. Present opening was fun. She knew this as she had already practised on some gifts that were already under the tree. Oh Cocoa!

"I'm pretty sure Father Christmas doesn't bring pets as Christmas presents poppet," Grandpa chirped as he licked his lips from his third mince pie.

"Anyway, you two, time for bed now. You don't want to be awake when the sleigh lands on the roof or you may not get any presents at all!"

"Okay Mum. Remember not to put any more logs on the fire thought, it needs to be fully out by the time Father Christmas comes down the chimney." Sam did worry about the practicalities of the expedition taking place that night.

The children were now tucked up in bed, and surprisingly, they were asleep. This Christmas Eve had taken then a little longer to drift off than usual because they had to give up Sam's room for Grandma and Grandpa to stay so had to share. Sam finally put an end to Sarah's nonstop talk about Father Christmas and his reindeer.

"I'm going to have as many dogs as Father Christmas has reindeer when I'm a big girl," she had announced. It was at this point Sam had said,

"Right, next one to speak doesn't get to go first opening presents!" Sarah immediately shot under the covers, closing her eyes tight and pressing her finger firmly over her lips to stop herself from talking. This was never an easy task, but amidst all the chatter and excitement, she was fast asleep in minutes.

"Thank goodness for that," thought Sam, "Peace at last," also drifting off to sleep quite quickly after this, his tummy turning somersaults at the thought of Christmas Day approaching. Yes, the presents were a bonus, but that feeling of all the family being together and the yummy food on offer all day long was his favourite part.

Meanwhile, the adults were downstairs enjoying a glass of sweet sherry when there was a firm tap on the front door.

"Who can this be so late on Christmas Eve?" quizzed Albert as he popped his glass on the coffee table and went to see who was at the door. "Oh, hi Jim. Come in."

Jim was Emily's dad. Emily hadn't been in school for the last two weeks of term as she still had a very sore leg and it had been making her cry - a lot. Vicky and Sarah had been over to their house most days after school and the girls would play and giggle while the two mums chatted over coffee. This made Emily very happy and cheered her up no end, having her best friend visit while she couldn't go to school. "Our mums look very deep in conversation, don't they?" she would say to Sarah. "Let's get up to some mischief like Cocoa while they aren't watching," she sniggered. Sarah would laugh and join in, doing anything her best friend wanted. She loved her so much.

Vicky looked up as Jim entered the room and smiled, pleased to see him. But only for a moment, as she saw the look on his face...

"Whatever is the matter?" asked Vicky, coming to the side of her husband and putting her hand into his for comfort.

As Jim came into the light in the living room, it was clear he was shocked about something. His face was flushed and his eyes were dark from what looked like lack of sleep.

"Sit down, we'll get you a sherry," Vicky insisted.

Vicky squeezed Albert's hand, reassuring him with a nod to make conversation, before she went to the kitchen for a glass. After a few deep breaths and sips of sherry, Jim started to speak, shakily at first. "It's our Emily. She's very poorly and has to go into hospital tonight. The doctors have said that her sore leg is more than just a strain from PE or growing pain and she needs to be seen by the hospital as soon as possible."

"Oh, dear me!" declared Vicky, who had been expecting this news from several chats with Martha and clasping her hands over her mouth continued, "How can we help you?" she said.

"Well, I know it's a lot to ask on Christmas Eve, but could you look after Scout until we know what is happening?"

Cocoa's ears pricked up as she awoke from her dreamworld. She had been so tired from the fun of the day, not even the tap on the door had woken her. Was this true? Was her best friend Scout going to be coming to stay for Christmas?

"Of course we can! He can stay as long as you need him to. Bring him in right away." Scout was sitting outside in the car wondering why he had been brought over to Cocoa's house so late at night, and on Christmas Eve. He was a nervous boy and would only stay with people he knew really well and in the company of certain other dogs. Well, only in the company of Cocoa should we say.

Jim went to his car and on opening the boot, scuffed up Scout's tuft of hair on his head and brought him into the house. He was delighted to see everybody, trotting round calmly, giving each person a lick in turn. He was a lot calmer than

Cocoa in social situations, which wasn't a hard task to beat. Scout eventually settled in the kitchen with Cocoa (who was still covered in glitter!) and Jim set off to the hospital to be with Emily and her mum, Martha.

"What are you doing here so late at night, Scout? Where are Amber and Digby?" woofed an interested and happy Cocoa, although could sense that this wasn't a totally cheery situation.

"My Emily has had to go to hospital," he replied with a tear appearing on the bottom lid of his left eye, "Amber and Digby have gone to our Auntie's house, but there was no room for me and I don't really get along too well with their other dogs. I get very nervous around them which makes me bark – Alot !! Anyway, I heard my mum say something about Emily being very poorly with a disease that begins with C but I can't remember what. She might be away from home for a few weeks."

"Come and share my basket, Scout - you're safe with us. We will look after you and you will get to have a Christmas dinner tomorrow. Extra gravy? Then my daddy will take us on a lovely long walk. It's all going to be alright. I'm here with you to comfort you and be beside you. No need to be scared or bark here."

"Thank you, Cocoa, you're a lovely friend," whimpered Scout as he snuggled down into the warm basket that was leaning against the oven door. "In fact, you're my very special "top of the list" friend Cocoa." These words melted Cocoa's heart and for once in her life she felt calm and settled in the knowledge she was able to be the strong one for her sorrowful friend.

Sherry glasses and crumbed plates from the mince pies were left on the coffee table as the adults all went upstairs with mixed feelings and thoughts, just in time for Father Christmas to deliver his gifts.

When morning came, the children couldn't contain themselves any longer. 6 a.m. seemed a respectable hour to be awake, so, after flinging back the winter duvets Mum had bought a few weeks earlier, they snook out of the bedroom, crept down the stairs and there was a pile of red, gold and green glittery wrapped presents.

“Morning, you two!” shouted the grandparents from the kitchen, with a whistle announcing that the kettle was boiling and the aroma of fresh bread toasting. Everybody was up already!

“It’s Christmas!” shouted Sam, “And Father Christmas has been.” Mum and Dad looked at each other, feeling blessed as their two happy children squealed in excitement. A tear appeared on Albert’s cheek as he thought of Emily in the hospital on Christmas morning – Vicky came behind him and wrapped her arms around his waist, feeling his sadness too.

“Mummy, Mummy come quick, there’s a dog in Cocoa’s basket and it’s not Cocoa.” Sarah looked on in shock and amazement. “I thought Father Christmas didn’t bring pets,” she continued, her voice rising in pitch in elation. Then, as she looked closer, she realised who it was. “Scout, is that you?” Four ears suddenly pricked up as Cocoa and Scout looked up from the basket. Cocoa licked Scout’s face with a reassuring sigh. Scout felt content after his cosy night’s sleep with his pal.

“We have some explaining to do, but first of all, let’s get that cup of tea and see what Father Christmas has brought,” said Vicky, clapping her hands together and kneeling next to the pile of gifts. Albert and Vicky weren’t looking forward to telling the children the reason Scout had shared Cocoa’s bed for the night and may have to continue for a few nights more.

As Christmas day passed by, as usual, it left the family feeling even more grateful for the precious friendships that were forming, both with humans and furry friends – relationships that are often overlooked and taken for granted.

Chapter Nine

Snow On the Farm

The recent lack of rain and the crisp air could only indicate one thing: snow was on its way. The winter seemed endless, with the cold weather continuing to linger. Anna had bounced into school that week, excited to share her news that she finally had her own puppy.

"Is it a border collie, Anna?" Sarah had asked, praying that her friend had got her dream dog.

"No, it's even better. It's my very own Patterdale Terrier called Poppy," Anna announced proudly. Sarah didn't know what sort of dog that was but was thrilled for her pal and had continued by asking when she could go for tea to meet Poppy the Patterdale.

"Of course, you'll be her very first guest." Anna had replied, "we'll be able to take our dogs for walks together, with Emily too hopefully soon when she is all better." Anna really did love dogs more than anything, even more than humans, and dreamed of being a vet one day.

Scout had spent three weeks with the Cooper family during the Christmas holidays and start of the term, but had returned home now that Emily was out of the hospital. She was still very poorly and had started taking tablets to help her feel better. It had been confirmed that Emily had the disease starting with C, which the dogs couldn't recall. Sarah was saddened by her friend's illness, causing her often to become lost in her own world. Lost in thought, she pictured herself having fun with Emily, her cheek resting against her hand. Emily enjoyed playing pranks on parents, and her lovely smile would always save her from getting in trouble.

Sarah found herself once again staring out the school window on a Friday, while Mrs Clarke taught addition and subtraction. Although Sarah enjoyed Maths class, her longing for her friend's presence was even greater.

Suddenly, there from the sky, it came. One, two, three ...

"It's snowing!" screamed Sarah. The whole class jumped up in excitement and ran to the window; Mrs Clarke rolled her eyes and tried desperately, but unsuccessfully, to calm the class down. As the snow thickened in the playground, the volume of the children's voices got louder and louder.

"Well, that's my teaching over for the day," she mused to herself.

"Come on then, let's get our coats on," she cried. "Would anyone like an extra playtime today?"

With cries of delight and fists pumping in the air, the class hurriedly grabbed their coats and shoes. Nobody really cared whether they had their own or not. Woolly hats were eagerly placed on excited heads and gloves were thrust on to tiny hands.

Outside, Sarah could see her brother busily gathering the bits of snow that had fallen to create snowballs. Sam glanced up and smiled at her through the window, using his wet glove to beckon her to come and play. It was coming down very, very heavily now. Within half an hour, half-constructed snowmen were created and snowballs were thrown, leaving icy imprints on coats. All the children were asked to come inside and continue the final hour of learning for the day, which involved a discussion on snow formation and ice safety, since the excitement was making it difficult to concentrate on maths.

"Now remember what I told you about the weekend and snow play. The ponds and lakes will be frozen, but you must not try to walk on them. The ice is thinner than it looks and you could fall through, and of course, that has very dangerous consequences." The children listened transfixed as this important speech came from Mrs Clarke. Each individual embraced her message, recognising her not only as a teacher, but as a compassionate person who cared deeply for them. They were totally right! Mrs Clarke had a great deal of love and care for them.

Once school was done, the snow had completely stuck to the ground and fields. The skies had provided enough white fun to go sledging over the weekend. A hill at the back of the farm led to the next farm, where there were many chickens and goats. By using a small gate on their farm, the children could quickly access the hill with their sledges. The shortcut was no secret to the school children, who would eagerly congregate at the front of Meaburn Hill Farm with flushed, excited faces from the cold. So as Saturday morning came...

"Come on in!" shouted Vicky to the hoards as they arrived. By now Cocoa was whimpering with excitement at the groups of children, at the snow and at the thought of racing down that big hill!

"Calm down, Cocoa." said Sam as he put his red scarf, hat and gloves on which were plain advertising for his favourite football team, "I'll take you up on the hill with us so you can come and play in the snow."

Just then, Emily and Anna arrived at the gate with Scout and Poppy. Sarah was thrilled to see both of them, especially Emily, as they hadn't been able to play together at school for a few weeks. "We've brought our dogs to play!" they announced. Cocoa was even more excitable now that she could see her two doggy friends waiting for her to play, too.

“Yippee!” Sarah screamed, “Come on Sam, bring Cocoa.”

“Oh no!” he thought to himself, “Three crazy dogs and three crazy girls. This could get chaotic!”

Just then, as if to save him, Ben came running and sliding towards the group of friends. "Come on everybody, let's go and take our sledges to the top of the hill. Last one to the top smells of rotten eggs." The three giddy girls, Sam, and the enthusiastic dogs, followed Ben out into the field.

There was a sense of quietness around Emily. Emily was generally not a quiet person. She looked at the four children, who smiled and wondered why. Was she still feeling very poorly? Was this dreadful sickness not showing any signs of improvement? “My mum says I have to be careful and I’ve not to get on the sledge,” mumbled Emily, looking to the ground with a sad lilt. Emily wasn’t pleased. “If I knock my leg, it could be very sore and very dangerous.”

"I'll stick around, Emily," Sam whispered. "Sledging doesn't really bother me."

Emily's face instantly brightened with a smile as she took Sam's arm and they all went to the field. Sam's face was now beetroot red. Emily was always teasing Sam, saying she would marry him one day. I guess you never know? Cocoa gazed at her brother Sam and pondered on the comment he had just made. "I'm sure I heard him say earlier how much he loved sledging. He always talks about being strong and brave. Surely he isn't scared..." she thought. But no, Sam wasn't scared. He was giving up his fun to look after his friend.

Ben, Sarah, and Anna ascended and descended the hill multiple times, with Cocoa, Scout, and Poppy joining in. The two girls squealed with delight as the dogs enthusiastically licked their faces, urging them to get up for the next run. Ben was much faster than them at getting up to the top of the magical slopes that glistened in the afternoon winter sun. Sam and Emily watched from the bottom, happily making the best snowman *ever* made. Like *ever*!

"It's finished – ta daaaaa!" declared Emily, throwing her arms in the air and looking very proud of their super snowman that stood just taller than her and just shorter than Sam. It was by far the best in the field. "It was so kind of you to use your favourite hat, scarf and gloves, Sam, to decorate our snowman. Just need to find the last few stones to put on his front to make the buttons for his coat."

Just as she made this announcement, Sam yelled, "Watch out!" Within seconds, three snow covered dogs came crashing into the masterpiece of a snowman, taking Sam and Emily with them into a heap of white powder.

"Ouch!" Sam shouted as he scrambled up off the ground. "Are you OK, Emily?" he asked with a worried look on his face and reaching his now frozen hand out to her. Sarah and Anna ran quickly, dragging their sledges behind them to join the chaos.

"My leg," cried a red and teary faced Emily, "I think we better get my dad."

The three dogs, now gathered up by the other two girls, sat looking sad and worried as they saw what they had done.

"We're going to be in huge trouble this time," barked Poppy.

"Oh yes we are!" Scout added while shivering in the cold and not looking forward to the thought of being scolded later.

"I'll run and get my dad," said Sarah, worried about her best friend. "He'll know what to do." Ben had now joined the group and ran with Sarah to get help.

A few minutes passed, but this felt like an hour to Emily, who was now in a lot of pain. In the distance, the children could see Albert and Sarah running over the snowy field. Emily's dad was just behind them with Ben.

"Come on, poppet," said Jim as he lovingly scooped his daughter up into his arms. "Let's get you home and see what the doctor has to say." He shot a worried glance towards Albert, who repeatedly apologised for the dogs' behaviour as he handed Scout over to his owner and took charge of Cocoa and Poppy on their leads. Scout looked back, tail between his legs, at his two chaotic companions. For once, Cocoa had no thoughts or words to sum this up. This was not a good day.

Sarah and Anna were both in tears, feeling immense sadness that, not only could their friend not join them in sledging, she was now hurt. In a show of solidarity, they held onto each other's hands as they journeyed back to the farmhouse.

"Actually, we'll keep Scout with us," said Albert, shaking Jim's hand. "He's more than welcome with us as long as you need us to have him."

Cocoa's sad heart leapt with joy and she and Scout beamed at each other; this was the best news. Doggy sleepovers, and maybe Poppy could stay too? But wait, what was going to happen to Emily? As the group walked down from the field to the house, each one had their own thoughts. Dogs and humans alike.

"Hot chocolate all round," came that reassuring voice that the whole family loved. "And hot milk for the doggies. There was Vicky at the door waiting to greet them all, no one feeling in trouble anymore – just loved.

Scout stayed at the farm with Cocoa for a few weeks after that and a wonderful friendship was developing, just like their humans. "I wonder why I'm still here," grumbled Scout one morning. His night had been unsettled and lack of sleep had made him grumpy.

"I think it's just because your family can't take you for big walks at the moment," said Cocoa, "Emily is still in the hospital with her sore leg and hip." Cocoa snuggled up to Scout in his bed which was now next to hers in front of the warm oven. "It'll all be OK, Scouty. You can stay here and have walks with me until your Emily is better."

Scout's spirits lifted as he leaned against Cocoa's back, feeling grateful for his amazing friend. "Cocoa, thank you. Although, I don't know if I feel much like big walks at the moment."

Just as Cocoa was about to answer, saying that walks are the best, she hesitated. Reflecting on Sam's past experience with Emily on the snow-covered hill, she came to a realisation. "I don't really care much for walks either, Scout. I'll stay with you," she whispered. Really precious lifelong friendships were developing – both for the dogs, adults and the children alike.

Chapter Ten

February Goodbyes

The day had finally come for Scout to go back home, and the family was feeling a combination of happiness and sadness as they prepared. The rain was coming down so forcefully that it bounced off the kitchen window ledge prior to landing on the ground. "Thank you for being my best friend, Cocoa. I've had a marvellous time and

I'm sure we'll get to play out again soon. I will miss our sleepovers." The two pals stared out at the miserable weather, feeling just about as miserable as themselves. "Not a good day for a walk today," sighed Cocoa. "Even I don't feel like getting muddy and wet today."

Within half an hour of their arrival, Jim and Martha came and went. No time for a cup of tea today. After Scout's car disappeared from view, Cocoa wearily made her way back inside the kitchen. She missed having Scout around and moped about, sniffing the floor slowly for tit-bits of food she may have missed.

"Chin up, Cocoa," said Vicky, "We all miss Scout being here too. He was a fun friend for you to have to stay, but we can take him out again soon for walks."

Despite trying, Scout couldn't recall the name of the disease that was causing Emily's illness. Cocoa could remember, though, and it was cancer. The children and their parents had many conversations, and now both understood why Emily had to spend so much time in the hospital. Sarah's continuous visits to Emily only made their relationship stronger. The doctors did everything they could to help Emily feel better and brought laughter to the girls when Sarah came to visit. The girls enjoyed pranking the nurses and once even pretended to leave the hospital by escaping from the ward. Emily was also starting to view the doctors and nurses as her special friends.

"When do you think Emily will get better Mum?" asked Sam in his grown-up voice as he sat by the fire with his Mum and Dad, watching it crackle and spark, "She's been poorly for a long time now."

Vicky swallowed, "Well, the doctors are doing lots of good things to help her and she's going to be going to America for three months soon to see some other doctors as well. They are the really clever ones who know how to treat this disease."

"Wow, America!" exclaimed Sam, leaning his head into his hands. He pictured travelling to these wonderful places that he'd only ever seen in books. He remembered the photographs he'd seen of his Mum and Dad visiting far away, wonderful places and thought about the adventures he'd love to have. Then he thought of Emily and the reason why she was travelling all that way. A lump formed in his throat. Sam thought it was a secret lump, but it seemed his Mum could see it as she said, "Remember, Sam, I know you want to be bold and strong, but letting your tears fall for the people you love is good. It means you've opened up your heart, that you have let people inside, and that is the bravest and strongest thing of all to do."

Sam gazed at his dad and saw a giant tear crash onto his father's lap. Leaning in to his dad's chest, he thought, "Yes, it's good to love and let people into our hearts." The three hugged in a way that each one of them knew what the other was thinking.

Sarah skipped into the room, bringing her fizzy joy with her, and asked, "So, if Emily is going to America, who is going to look after the dogs?"

"Amber is going to her auntie in Brighton. Digby is going to another auntie in Scotland and Scout, well there aren't any other relatives to have him, so he will have to go into boarding kennels," replied Vicky.

"Kennels?" both children shrieked at the same time, "Mummy, no, no, he can't go to the kennels! We never send Cocoa there, so Scout won't like it either." Sarah continued to protest.

"Kennels?" Cocoa thought to herself and started to whimper loudly at the doom her friend faced. "It may be ok for some dogs, but Scout won't like it knowing how he likes his home comforts."

"See, even Cocoa knows what you're saying, and she doesn't approve!" Sam crossed his arms and stamped his foot.

"There's nothing that can be done. The decision has been made. Martha and Jim have enough to think about, and Scout is going there tomorrow afternoon. He isn't our dog and we can't make decisions and demands about where he goes. Now, no more talking about this; it's only making you both very sad."

"Both!" thought Cocoa, her heart breaking inside. "Sam, Sarah and me... that's three! I love Scout more than any of you."

The rest of that day was a very rainy, quiet one. The family was feeling sad about Emily leaving for a long time and Scout going to boarding kennels. Even Cocoa lay quietly for once in front of the fire; she didn't even move when the tea cake crumbs fell from Albert's lap on to the threadbare rug. Cocoa was going to miss her walks with her pal while he was away.

Night time came and passed and the morning brought fresh light to a brand new day. With the sun breaking through, the farm felt a bit more hopeful this morning. The rain had eased overnight, but showers were still in the air. Vicky switched on the radio, twisting the control button to find the correct channel among the echoing scratchy noises. The house was filled with beautiful music, bringing joy to the hearts of the two children who had been so sad the previous night. She sang along. Vicky had always wanted to be a singer on the stage in New York. She pictured what that would be like, and a smile broke across her face. Singing in a silly voice, she swayed and pretended to be part of the famous shows, dancing along. As she spun round, there they were, the rest of the family smiling back at her, breaking her fantasy with a giggle. Albert grabbed her waist tightly and spun her round until she nearly fell over. All four of them were now belly laughing as Albert pulled faces and sang in a silly voice. Cocoa jumped up at them, each in turn at all the musical merriment being made, barking as she lept.

The giddiness of the kitchen calmed down, eventually. "Breakfast anyone?" Vicky continued while humming the tune, as her cheeks flushed. 'Oh what a beautiful morning!' she sang as she reached high into the cupboard to get the bowls for cereal, "Weetabix, Sugar Puffs, Cornflakes?"

Squeezing his wife's waist as he did a "dad" dance past her towards the fridge to get the milk out, Albert now joined in the merry tune.

"You two are very jolly this morning," smiled Sarah.

"It's weird!" announced an embarrassed Sam, burying his head into his hands.

Just as he was about to ask his parents to stop this nonsense, Cocoa started to bark, louder than ever before. The gravel scattered as she heard a car pulling up on to the drive outside the kitchen door.

"Who could this be?" said Albert, with a smirk and a wink at his wife, "Well, you two better go and look while me and Mum finish sorting breakfast," he announced, pointing towards the window and back door.

Flinging the door open so wildly that it banged into the wall behind, Sam and Sarah stood, mouths wide open. Cocoa bolted past them into the garden, not caring that it was still raining, and then continued in a frenzy over to the car that had now parked. Jim jumped out of the driver's seat and...

"It's Emily!" screamed Sarah.

"And, and... Scout!" cried Sam.

"Thank you so much for saying you'll look after Scout while I go away." Emily beamed, "I am so happy he's staying with my bestest friend in the whole world." Sam and Cocoa shot a quick glance at Albert who stood grinning. The phone call last night to Emily's parents had been worth the surprise that came this morning. The two girls hugged and cried as they were going to miss each other so much. How on earth will they cope without each other for twelve whole weeks? It would feel like twelve years to them. Sam coughed as he felt his eyes fill with tears. At first, he swallowed hard to hold them back, but then he remembered what his Mum had said. He wrapped his arms around the two girls and did the bravest and strongest thing of all – the salty tears flowed down his cheeks, leaving traces on his new stripy blue jumper.

"Oh my, it's stopped raining, but it's raining tears, cats and dogs here! Mainly dogs," Emily joked, and the children all fell to the floor laughing, stumbling over each other, still hugging.

Cocoa couldn't contain her excitement any longer. She bounced and jumped up and began to chase Scout around the garden.

"I'm so happy you are back, buddy!" she woofed, licking Scout's face until he fell over.

"I'm so happy to be back, friend! Who knows how long I'll be here this time but we are going to make the most of it." he replied, "Hey, they all look distracted...where did you say that secret stash of biscuits is kept?"

The two dogs ran towards the kitchen door. Vicky and Albert were filled with pride as they waited there for their children, who had embraced the value of love for others. Their growth was not in size, but in their ability to treat people and bring joy to their lives. Life surely could be hard, even at a young age. Unable to contain them any longer, Vicky's bottom lids brimmed with two shimmering tears, reflecting the newfound friendships that were blossoming and strengthening daily. She blinked and they rolled on to her pink hot cheeks. Albert pulled his wife close to his chest saying, "Let's get the kettle on, the children will be in shortly." This was his way of saying, "They need time to say their goodbyes to their friend. They can handle this." And yes, they could.

While heading inside, Vicky noticed a striking burst of colour. In the sky, a breathtakingly beautiful rainbow could be seen. "This is truly a remarkable symbol of hope and love," she smiled, "we are all so truly blessed to have each other. Not just the humans, but the dogs, too." – and the tears began to flow again. This time happy ones. Out of nowhere, a white and brown puff ball dashed through the house with an enthusiastic Cocoa in pursuit. "Here comes Scout!" they both said at the same time and laughed. What adventures would the next few weeks bring? Without a doubt, they were going to be memories worth remembering.

Here Comes Scout

Book Two Teaser

"Emily, can you tell me what time you'll be landing in the UK?" Sarah held onto every word of her best friend's phone call from America with excitement. The months of being apart had been hard on the two friends, who were now desperate to be together again. Nestled beside Cocoa's bed, Scout's ears perked up from his blue and cream bed in front of the oven.

"Cocoa, did you hear that?" whispered an excited Scout in to his friend's ear. Two days left until Emily returns home, and then I'll be going back, too.

The pair of fluffy friends, who had developed a strong connection over the past few months, felt a mix of emotions. The return of Scout's family was incredible, but it also brought a touch of sadness, as the companions would be separated again.

Emily couldn't wait to go back home and by Saturday lunchtime, she would see Sarah and Scout. America had been difficult for her while she was in the hospital and receiving cancer treatment.

We can pause the story right here. How about we take a trip back in time to a few months ago and find out what went on while Emily was away and Scout became part of Sam, Sarah, and Cocoa's lives?

As the cold morning dawned on the farm, snowdrops emerged from the dewy grass in front of the farmhouse. To be continued ....

Printed in Great Britain
by Amazon

59453830R00069